HOSPITAL SHIPS &
TROOP TRANSPORTS OF
THE FIRST WORLD WAR

HOSPITAL SHIPS & TROOP TRANSPORTS OF THE FIRST WORLD WAR

Campbell McCutcheon

AMBERLEY

First published 2015

Amberley Publishing
The Hill, Stroud
Gloucestershire, GL5 4EP

www.amberley-books.com

British Library Cataloguing in Publication Data.
A catalogue record for this book is available from the British Library.

ISBN 978 1 4456 3867 6 (print)
ISBN 978 1 4456 3884 3 (ebook)

Typesetting and Origination by Amberley Publishing.
Printed in Great Britain.

CONTENTS

	Introduction	7
1	Allan Line, Canadian Pacific and Canadian Northern	20
2	Australian and New Zealand Lines	29
3	British India Steam Navigation Co.	37
4	Cunard	46
5	Orient Line	57
6	Peninsular & Oriental Steam Navigation Co.	62
7	Railway Steamers	71
8	Royal Indian Marine Service	75
9	Royal Mail Steam Packet Co.	81
10	Union-Castle Line	88
11	White Star Line	94
12	Other British Lines	110
13	Muirhead Bone, War Artist	125

INTRODUCTION

The use of merchant vessels both to carry soldiers to and from conflict zones and to take wounded personnel back to major hospitals is not new. Many passenger vessels were taken up during the Crimean War to take troops to the Black Sea. Again, during the Boer War, British merchant ships were called up for military duty, taking troops on the 6,000-mile trip from Southampton to the Cape. Those who could not be attended to in South African hospitals were brought home in hospital ships, fitted out with the needs of a modern hospital.

The history of hospital ships can roughly be dated to 1859 and the Battle of Solferino, between the French and Austrian armies. A Swiss businessman called Jean Henri Dunant saw the aftermath of the battle and set about the founding of the International Red Cross, as well as the Geneva Conventions, a series of agreements between major nations as to the treatment of non-combatants, civilians and wounded soldiers in wartime. The First Geneva Convention was signed by twelve European countries in 1864 and the Red Cross had been founded. This first convention was for soldiers on land, where most major battles were fought at the time. The second convention, of 1906, covered warfare at sea, something that had changed greatly from the time of the first convention with the transition from wooden-walled sailing ships and steamships, fitted with cannon only capable of close action and fitted for broadside actions only, to modern battleships and shells that could be fired ten miles or more. By 1906, the age of the Dreadnought was upon us, and traversing turrets, steel hulls, turbine machinery and the submarine had brought huge changes in the ability of ships to destroy each other. It was this year that saw the introduction of the Second Geneva Convention, covering both soldiers and sailors at sea, and setting out rules for the transport of wounded combatants.

During the Crimean War, many troop transports were simply passenger vessels from Britain's major shipping lines taken up for service and used for the transport of troops rather than civilians. Ships of the Peninsular & Oriental Steam Navigation Co., of the British & North American Royal Mail Steam Packet Co. (or Cunard Line), and the Royal Mail Steam Packet Co. bore the brunt of the transport and the use of their ships for around three years had a huge impact on their trade. However, the ships were under charter so each company was still making money, despite the disruption to their trade. By the end of the war, they were building larger and faster ships.

The Boer War, with its logistical difficulties for Britain, was to see many ships chartered as troopships, to carry the tens of thousands of troops who would be needed to fight the Boers, the native Dutch settlers. With an average transit time of over three weeks, it was important to get British troops to the conflict zone as quickly as possible. Ships of the Union Line, Castle Line, Cunard, White Star, P&O, British India, Allan Line, Royal Mail Steam Packet Co. and numerous other shipping lines were taken up for service to become Her Majesty's Troopships, with the designation HMT. From 1899 to 1902, British ships were used in large numbers to transport troops to the Cape. The first month or two of the war saw British troops hurriedly shipped to Africa and major offensives did not start until the end of January. By 1 September, the British deemed the war almost over, with the Transvaal annexed and much of the land taken by the Boers recaptured. Some 50,000 British troops were in the colony and the Boers changed tack, using small groups to attack, using guerilla tactics to disrupt the British troops. This resulted in a fifteen-month period that tied up even more troops, all of whom needed to be transported from Britain or India. Eventually, after a scorched earth policy, the Boers were brought to the negotiating table and the war was over in May 1902. Thousands of troops were then shipped back home, along with the wounded, who were transported in ships painted all-over white with red crosses along their sides. The generosity of Bernard Baker, president of Atlantic Transport Co., saw their ship *Maine* being offered to the navy in 1899. It was converted into a hospital ship, the navy's first dedicated one, and saw service with the Royal Fleet Auxiliary until it was wrecked on the coast of Mull in 1914.

The construction of two giant new Cunard liners was made possible by a government loan that saw the ships designed in such a way that they could be converted in times of war into armed merchant cruisers, passenger liners with guns. These two giants, *Lusitania* and *Mauretania*, were not the first Cunarders to be capable of conversion into armed warships, nor were they the first British liners capable of being converted. In 1889, the White Star liner RMS *Teutonic* appeared at the Spithead naval review, sporting guns. She was the very first British armed merchant cruiser, and was built under the British Auxiliary Armed Cruiser Agreement, and sported eight 4.7-inch guns. The British Admiralty had realised early on that the ability both to arm and use merchant ships for trooping purposes meant that they would not need ships tied up for much of the year unused and could simply 'borrow' them from British shipping lines as and when required. During their construction, many ships, and most notably *Lusitania* and *Mauretania*, were subsidised under this agreement between the Admiralty and their owners.

After the Kaiser had seen the *Teutonic* at the Spithead review, and inspected her for some two hours, he set Germany on a course that saw a huge expansion of both her naval and merchant fleets. The Germans introduced the first four-funnel liners, again all designed to be used as warships or troopships in wartime. The first decade of the twentieth century saw an arms race between Britain and Germany that spilled over into the merchant fleets. The growth of both Britain and Germany's navies came with a commensurate growth in the merchant fleets. The naval arms race pushed the two countries towards war. The spark would be the murder of Archduke Franz Ferdinand in Sarajevo, and it would ignite the world. The British mobilised and the British Expeditionary Force was sent to France, primarily on cross-Channel ferries, and ships were called up for military service. Literally hundreds of vessels were used as troopships and hospital ships, sometimes for a single voyage, more often through whole years or for the duration. The global nature of the conflict meant that troops were sent from all over the Empire to France, but they were also sent to Asia, Africa, the Middle East, the Pacific and the South Atlantic. They had to be transported and the injured had to be recovered back home, whether that home was the United Kingdom, Canada, Australia, New Zealand, India, South Africa or even Fiji or Grenada.

Within the following pages you will find just some of the troopships and hospital ships used in the conflict. Most managed to survive the war and re-entered civilian service once more, but some were lost to mine, torpedo, navigational error or were simply worn out after their war service. However, even hospital ships, supposedly immune to enemy action, were targeted. Sunk by submarine and hit by mine, a reasonable number of hospital ships succumbed. Each loss created an outrage at the time and two German officers were even charged by a German court for the war crime of sinking a hospital ship. The world's biggest wartime loss, the HMHS *Britannic*, still lies in 400 feet of water in the Kea Channel, almost perfectly preserved as a reminder of the folly of war. Hit by a mine, she sank in less than an hour. However, the vast majority of ships did survive, and they performed a hugely important role in ensuring the wounded were cared for and the vast majority got home safely. While many ships are not covered here, it is a factor of space that sees them missing. Enjoy what there is, and let those who did not arrive safely home be remembered too for the sacrifice they made for us.

One of Britain's most famous war poets died aboard a hospital ship, anchored off the Greek island of Skyros, at 4.46 p.m. on 23 April 1915. Rupert Brooke died not of wounds received but of a mosquito bite. His poem 'The Soldier' is a fitting epitaph for many soldiers and sailors who were tended by the nurses aboard the hospital ships that served the British, Canadian, Australian, New Zealand, Indian and African troops who fought for freedom.

If I should die, think only this of me:
That there's some corner of a foreign field
That is forever England. There shall be
In that rich earth a richer dust concealed;
A dust whom England bore, shaped, made aware,
Gave, once, her flowers to love, her ways to roam,
A body of England's, breathing English air,
Washed by the rivers, blest by the suns of home.
And think, this heart, all evil shed away,
A pulse in the eternal mind, no less
Gives somewhere back the thoughts by England given;
Her sights and sounds; dreams happy as her day;
And laughter, learnt of friends; and gentleness,
In hearts at peace, under an English heaven.

Britain's first naval hospital ship was the Royal Fleet Auxiliary *Maine*. The ship was built in 1887 as the *Swansea* and was offered to the navy during the Boer War. *Maine* sailed for South Africa in December 1899, and then headed to China for duties during the Boxer Rebellion. In 1901, the ship was being used as a hospital ship in the Mediterranean. She was lost, just before the war started, on the island of Mull (as shown here) on 17 June 1914 and sold for scrap on 6 July. She would be one of the first of many vessels used by the navy as a hospital ship.

Soldiers would be brought from the Front in France and Belgium by hospital trains, many of which were supplied by British railway companies, with specially made trains being built at Horwich, Swindon and Glasgow in 1915 and 1916 for hospital service.

A hospital ship being loaded at Le Havre. Many tens of thousands of wounded soldiers would be brought back to Blighty via converted ferries and ocean liners before being transported by train all over the country.

The soldiers would be transported by hospital train from Dover, Folkestone or Southampton to Voluntary Aid Detachment (or VAD) hospitals throughout the UK. This view of the Beaufort War Hospital in Bristol is typical of many taken during the war years of convalescing soldiers.

Above: The First World War was the first major conflict to involve so many countries, with fighting in Africa, Asia, the South Atlantic, the Pacific, the Middle East and Europe. It required the movement of men in numbers never seen before, as well as the need for hospital ships to transport the wounded back home. This view shows a British hospital ship at Aden, *c.* 1917.

Right: Thousands of nurses were required to tend the wounded, often moving between hospital ships as and when they were required. These nurses were photographed aboard the Italian hospital ship *Re D'Italia* at Malta on 23 September 1915.

In their leisure time, the nurses would entertain themselves and the troops.
Shown here at Floriana Hospital, Malta, are nurses in floats decorated as two
hospital ships.

Even those at home recognised the need for hospital ships. This is a float from a war week fundraising parade in south-eastern England, built over the body of a tram and used to parade the streets.

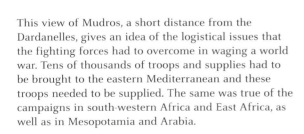

This view of Mudros, a short distance from the Dardanelles, gives an idea of the logistical issues that the fighting forces had to overcome in waging a world war. Tens of thousands of troops and supplies had to be brought to the eastern Mediterranean and these troops needed to be supplied. The same was true of the campaigns in south-western Africa and East Africa, as well as in Mesopotamia and Arabia.

A troopship leaves Southampton for a battle zone half way around the world.

Closer to home, the War Department tender *Satellite* is crowded with soldiers.

Some ships were too big to risk close to the battlefields so smaller vessels were used to shift the wounded from the Front to a safe distance away, where they could be trans-shipped.

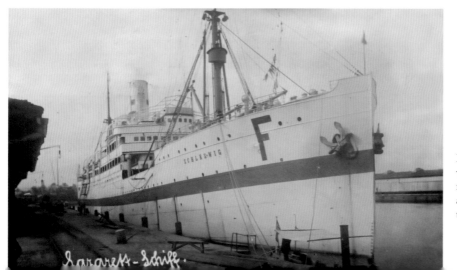

Let us not forget that the enemy also required hospital ships. These vessels were protected under the Geneva Conventions but the Germans managed to sink numerous hospital ships, by both torpedo and mine, in at least one case attempting to kill all those who had survived by shelling their lifeboats.

Above and right: At the end of the war, the Royal Navy recognised the need for a permanent hospital ship and fleet auxiliary and used the *Panama*, an ex-hospital ship, and renamed her *Maine*, after the first hospital ship of the Royal Navy. After the Second World War, the Royal Yacht *Britannia* was designed to be converted into a hospital ship if needed.

ALLAN LINE, CANADIAN PACIFIC AND CANADIAN NORTHERN

Launched on 22 March 1913 at the yard of William Beardmore, Glasgow, when the Allan Line was effectively owned by Canadian Pacific Line, the *Alsatian* left on her maiden voyage from Liverpool to Halifax and St John, New Brunswick, on 17 January 1914. She remained in commercial service at the start of the war but was taken up for military service in September 1914. She was the flagship of the 10th Cruiser Squadron.

The *Alsatian* leaving Canada for Europe with troops from Valcartier Camp. The *Alsatian* and her sister, *Calgarian*, were the first passenger ships to sail the Atlantic with cruiser sterns.

The Allan Line's *Pretorian* was built in Hartlepool in 1901. She made numerous trooping voyages during the First World War. She was scrapped in 1926.

Left: The *Scandinavian* was built by Harland & Wolff for the Dominion Line in 1898 and launched as RMS *New England.* Bought by the Allan Line in 1912, she did numerous trooping voyages during the war and is shown here en route to Canada from Southampton. Her paintwork is dulled down.

Below: Allan Line's RMS *Scotian* was originally built in 1898 as the *Statendam* for Holland America Line. She was purchased by the Allan Line in 1911 and renamed *Scotian.* In 1914, she served as a troopship and did so again at the war's end, taking soldiers back to Canada from the UK. She is shown here outside Southampton's International Cold Store at berth 39. She was renamed *Marglen* in 1922.

Allan Line's *Virginian* was launched on 22 December 1904 at Alexander Stephens' yard, Linthouse, and entered service on 6 April 1905. At the start of the war she was taken over for trooping and made voyages from Canada to the UK. In November 1914, she was taken up for conversion into an armed merchant cruiser and attached to the 10th Cruiser Squadron. She spent much of the war between the American east coast seaboard and the western approaches of the United Kingdom. Her four bow guns are clearly shown here, as is the super dazzle paint scheme, designed to confuse U-boats. She was sold to the Swedish America Line and renamed *Drottningholm* in 1920. During the Second World War, she was used by the Red Cross for exchange of wounded prisoners of war.

The *Empress of Asia* was built as a transpacific liner for Canadian Pacific in 1912. Registered at Vancouver, she served at the start of the war as an armed merchant cruiser. She returned to CPR service in 1916 but was taken over again in 1918 as a North Atlantic troopship and made six voyages across the Atlantic that year. She was used at the war's end to repatriate Australian troops and is shown here in the Gatun Locks of the Panama Canal in late 1918. She made her way to Hong Kong afterwards and refitted for passenger service.

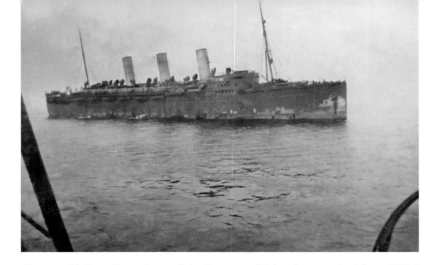

Above and below: Four views of the *Empress of Asia*, photographed from USS *Louisville*, when she was a North Atlantic troopship, used to bring American soldiers to France. When America entered the war in 1917, there was a huge push to bring as many soldiers across the Atlantic as possible. By early 1918, tens of thousands of American troops were pouring into France each month. She was used as a troopship during the Second World War too, and was sunk by Japanese aircraft during the Fall of Singapore.

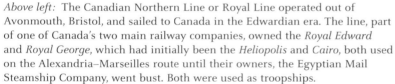

Above left: The Canadian Northern Line or Royal Line operated out of Avonmouth, Bristol, and sailed to Canada in the Edwardian era. The line, part of one of Canada's two main railway companies, owned the *Royal Edward* and *Royal George*, which had initially been the *Heliopolis* and *Cairo*, both used on the Alexandria–Marseilles route until their owners, the Egyptian Mail Steamship Company, went bust. Both were used as troopships.

Above right and below right: Two views taken aboard the *Royal Edward* while she was serving as a troopship. The troops are being kept entertained with wrestling and walking the promenade deck.

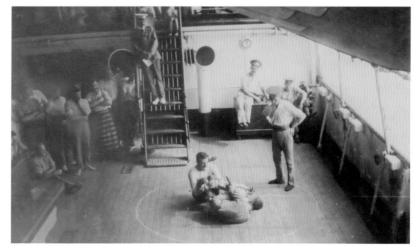

Farewell, "Royal Edward."

O! how often through the purple mists
   That clothe the coming night
I have seen the "Royal Edward"
   Pass, and vanish from my sight.
I have watched her glide where shadows lie,
   A world upon the sea;
I have said, "God speed the noble ship,
   That takes my love from me."
And now—her cargo, not of gold,
   But of metal greater far,—
She has taken England's noblest sons,
   And with them crossed the Bar.
O! Weep not for our heroes,
   For God Himself has said
"Lay down thy life for others,"
   So weep not for our dead—
Weep for the cowards, the careless,
   Weep that spies should mar our land,
And rise, and rouse, and wake yourselves,
   Hold out a loving hand
To every man in khaki,
   But let the cowards feel
That honest scorn will reach as far
   As the finest tempered steel.
So sleep, and wake in Paradise,
   Dear hearts beneath the sea,
And just one tear for the noble form
   That will ne'er come back to me.

Clevedon.   PETRONELLA O'DONNELL.

HMT *Royal Edward* was one of the bigger shipping losses of the First World War. She had been used to bring Canadian troops to the UK, and was then used as an internment ship at Southend-on-Sea. She embarked 1,367 troops at Avonmouth on 28 July 1915, and headed for Gallipoli. She arrived in Alexandria on 10 August and she then sailed for Mudros. On the morning of 13 August, she passed the P&O hospital ship *Soudan*. Both had been spotted by the U-boat *UB-14* but the *Soudan* was allowed to pass safely. A torpedo was fired as *Royal Edward* sailed off Kandeloussa. It hit the laden troopship in the stern and she sank in six minutes. A boat drill had just taken place and many men were down below, stowing their equipment. The *Soudan* returned and rescued 440 men but over 860 were lost, according to the Admiralty. This postcard was printed after the sinking.

The *Royal George* at Marseilles as a troopship. The *George* was luckier than her sister and survived the war, even if their owners did not. She was sold to Cunard in 1916 and operated as a troopship throughout the war.

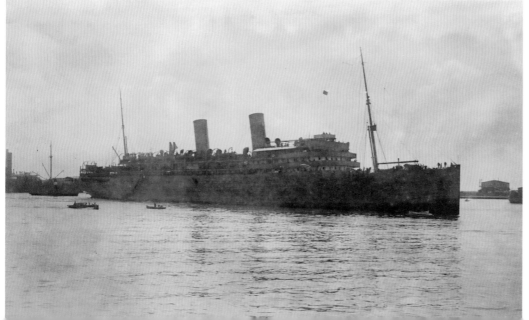

The *Royal George* at Port Said, with elements of the Naval Brigade aboard, on 28 March 1915. The men would be landing on the beaches at Gallipoli in early April. The *Royal George* was a top-heavy ship and was nicknamed the 'Rolling George'. Cunard used her for only a few voyages post-war and she was quickly relegated to being a floating hostel for emigrants at Cherbourg. She was scrapped in 1922 at Wilhelmshaven.

AUSTRALIAN AND NEW ZEALAND LINES

Australian Transport A14, *Euripides*. Designed for the route from London to Brisbane, *Euripides* made a shakedown cruise in June 1914 and then sailed for Brisbane. She left on 1 July and by the time she arrived in Brisbane on 24 August the war had been going on for over three weeks. She was instantly commandeered and became the commodore's ship of the very first Australian troop convoy to Europe. During the war she sailed 208,307 miles and carried 38,439 troops. In 1919 she repatriated troops back to Australia. She remained in commercial service during the Second World War and was finally scrapped in 1954 at Antwerp.

Above: The Aberdeen White Star liner *Miltiades* was built in 1903 by Alexander Stephen's at Glasgow and was of 6,793 grt. She was designed for the Aberdeen Line's route to Australia. Initially with a single funnel, she had a dummy fore-funnel added in 1912. During the war she spent most of her time trooping and is shown here leaving New York in a dazzle paint scheme on 19 May 1918. Many ships had been taken off the Australian trooping routes as the demands of the Americans increased in 1918 as they pushed to send as many men to Europe as possible.

Below: Built for Houlder Bros, the *Limerick* was owned by the start of the First World War by the Union Steamship Company of New Zealand. Her first trooping voyage was with parts of the NZ Field Artillery Brigade and Wellington Infantry Battalion, comprising 495 men and 348 horses. She was sunk by the U-boat *U-86* off Bishop's Rock on 28 May 1917.

Right: Built by Caird of Greenock in 1907, the *Marama* was the Union Line's largest and most expensive ship, at £166,000. Until 1915, she remained on her New Zealand to San Francisco route but was commandeered as a hospital ship in December 1915. Along with *Maheno*, another of the company's ships, she carried 47,000 men over fifteen voyages. Each was capable of carrying 550 patients at a time. In late 1919 she was decommissioned and returned to company service.

Below: The *Marama* in Auckland during the war. The danger of being sunk was lessened in the Pacific and Indian oceans after the loss of Germany's commerce raiders in the area.

Above: The *Niagara* of the Union Steamship Company of New Zealand remained in commercial service for the war but is shown here dulled down with grey paint during the war period. Built by John Brown, Clydebank, she was the first passenger ship built for oil burning and never revisited the UK after she left on her maiden voyage.

Left: One of twelve Union Steamship Company of New Zealand vessels used for war service, the *Tofua* was built in 1908 by William Denny at Dumbarton. She was 350 feet long and equipped with two triple-expansion engines. She was intended for the inter-island routes in the Pacific and cost £100,297. She is seen here, photographed from an aeroplane, in dazzle paint scheme in 1917–18.

Above: The Australian United Steam Navigation Company vessel *Kanowna* was used as both a troop ship and a hospital ship. She was requisitioned as a troopship on 8 August 1914 while at Townsville, Queensland. Between 1 and 6 June 1915, she was refitted at Cockatoo Island, Sydney, to carry 1,100 troops but on arrival in Britain was again converted to a 452-patient hospital ship. She spent the remainder of the war transporting wounded soldiers from the UK to Australia.

Right: The HMAT *Karroo* is shown here leaving Port Melbourne, Victoria, on 18 September 1916. After the Battle of the Somme and the disastrous Gallipoli campaign, men were still needed in huge quantities. The *Karroo* sailed on Australian Troop Convoy No. 24, via Port Natal, Dakar, Senegal, and Plymouth.

Above: The Australian shipping lines and their agents were very proud of the war service of their troopships. This advert postcard of HMAT A.10 was issued by W. G. Deuchar of Loftus Street, Sydney. The HMAT A10 *Karroo* weighed 6,127 tons and had an average speed of 12 knots. The ship was owned by the British Ellerman & Bucknall SS Co. Ltd, London, and was leased by the Australians until 3 January 1917.

Left: Owned by McIlwraith, McEacharn's Line of Melbourne, the *Karoola* was used as both a troopship and a hospital ship during the First World War. Her trooping number was A63. She was fully manned by Australian officers and crew and was leased to the Commonwealth until June 1919, when she returned to commercial service.

Opposite above: The *Wahehe* was originally built for the Woermann Line of Hamburg. At the end of the war, she was surrendered to the Allies and made three trooping voyages repatriating soldiers to Australia in 1919. She was managed by the Shaw, Savill Line and is shown here in Sydney, flying the Armistice flag.

Opposite below: Troops were repatriated by the *Armagh*, arriving back in Sydney on 16 May 1919. The troops were all South Australians and the *Armagh* carried 224 soldiers back home. The weather was rough on her arrival and rather than unload the soldiers by launch, they used the deck of the *War Viper* to get to the dockside, slowing the loading of wheat onto the *War Viper*.

Above left: The SS *Indarra* was owned by the Australasian United Steam Navigation Company of Fremantle. She is shown here at Sydney on one of the many repatriation voyages of Australian troops in 1919.

Above right: Built for the Adelaide Steamship Company, the *Wandilla* ordinarily operated on the Fremantle–Sydney service. In 1915, she became HMAT *Wandilla* and was used for trooping. In 1916, she was converted into a hospital ship. At the end of the war, she was returned to the Adelaide Steamship Company, and was sold to the Bermuda & West Indies Steamship Company.

Another German ship surrendered to the Allies was the *Windhuk*, shown here in 1919 in Sydney, having repatriated a thousand or more Australian troops back from France.

BRITISH INDIA STEAM NAVIGATION CO.

Shown here in her Boer War trooping days, the *Dunera* was built in 1891 by A. & J. Inglis, Glasgow, for British India service. She was initially used on the Queensland route but in 1892 was transferred to the London–Calcutta service. In 1896, she began trooping during the trooping season to India and, in 1900, made five return voyages to South Africa during the Boer War. On 16 October 1914, she brought much-needed Indian troops from Bombay to Southampton. During the war she made numerous trooping voyages and in 1918 was placed on the commercial Bombay–Japan run, being scrapped in Japan in 1922.

Elephanta was built in 1911 by Barclay, Curle, of Glasgow, and the 5,929 grt ship entered service in May of that year. In September 1914 she was trooping from Bombay to Marseille. In November 1914, she was used in the Basra river landings in Mesopotamia, then Turkish-held. She spent much of the war involved in the Iraqi conflict, spending 1917–21 trooping between Basra and Karachi. She took much-needed reinforcements to the conflict zone in 1917.

A view of *Elephanta* at Basra, landing reinforcements in 1917.

KARACOLA - 7,053 GR. TONS.
KARAPARA - 7,117 "
KAROA - 7,009 "

(The Karapara is here shown in war garb as a Hospital Ship.)

Right: Built on the Tyne, at Swan, Hunter & Wigham Richardson, in 1914, the *Karapara* was originally to have been named *Karunga*. With delays caused by the war and essential materials being used for warships, *Karapara* was not completed until 21 August 1915, when she was registered as a hospital ship, No. 17, and equipped with 341 beds and 200 medical staff. Based in Alexandria, she sailed for Gallipoli on 26 August 1915.

Below: In 1916, on 26 May, HMHS *Dover Castle* was sunk. Carrying 632 patients, over 270 were evacuated and taken by HMHS *Karapara* to Gibraltar.

Above left: Karapara was at Scapa Flow, Orkney, in April 1918 and later in the year was to be seen in the eastern Mediterranean again. During the summer of 1919, she provided medical facilities in Constantinople and was returned to BISNC in 1920. She was a hospital ship again during the Second World War, as No.36, with 338 beds and 123 medical staff. She was attacked while at Tobruk in her hospital ship colours on 4 May 1942. Towed to safety, she was repaired and not scrapped until 1950 in Bombay.

Above right: British India's HMT *Karoa* at Taranto, 1918. Entering service in March 1915, she was instantly fitted out as a troopship. In September 1915, she was damaged by gunfire from the Turkish batteries at Suvla Bay. In 1919, she repatriated Belgian refugees from England to Antwerp. She became a hospital ship during the Second World War.

Opposite above and below: Built by Barclay, Curle of Glasgow in 1914 for BISNC, *Merkara* was of 8,228 grt. Initially, she entered regular service on the London–Bombay route, as so many BISNC vessels had been taken up for trooping. In 1917, she was taken over under the Liner Requisition Scheme and suffered damage to her bottom when she hit a rock off the coast of Italy. She re-entered BISNC service at the end of the war and was scrapped in 1934 in Italy. *Margha,* her sister, was constructed in 1917 and took the name of a previous BISNC ship, which had been requisitioned by the Admiralty and converted into a fleet oiler named *Boxleaf.*

The two most famous BISNC troopships were also their largest ships when built in 1912 in Glasgow. The *Neuralia* and *Nevasa* were both of approximately 9,080 grt and were used on the London–Calcutta service pre-war. *Neuralia*, shown here at Southampton, with two funnels of the White Star Line's *Olympic* behind, was used on a voyage from Calcutta to Marseilles, leaving on 16 October 1914, carrying troops to bolster the Allied defences against the German onslaught of the autumn of that year. She was used again at Gallipoli as a troopship, and then converted to a hospital ship of 630 beds. She served between the eastern Mediterranean and Indian Ocean until March 1916, when she was based in the UK. In November 1918, she became an ambulance transport. She lasted as a troopship during the Second World War but was mined in the dying days of the war in Europe, on 1 May. Ironically, she hit an Italian mine, a country that by then was on the Allied side against the Germans.

Nevasa, sister of *Neuralia*, was launched on 12 December 1912 and entered service in March 1913, leaving on her maiden voyage from the UK via East Africa to Calcutta on 22 March 1913. She was requisitioned in August 1914 as a troopship and became a hospital ship in January 1915. She had accommodation for 660 beds. In August 1916, she was used in the East African and Persian Gulf campaigns and was at Iraq and Salonica, Greece, during campaigns in 1917.

Right and below: On 14 July 1918 and 2 October 1918, she was chased by submarines while being used as a troopship in the North Atlantic. Her speed and a smoke screen saw her escape both times. Between the wars she was converted into an educational ship and as a permanent troopship. She is shown below in Southampton with many of her lifeboats in the water, for drill. She was used as a troop ship during the Second World War, seeing action in Normandy and in the Pacific. In 1946, she reverted to BISNC and was used as a troopship until being scrapped in 1948 at Bo'ness, Scotland.

One of a pair of ships built by William Denny, at Dumbarton, HMT *Rewa* was completed on 6 June 1906 and made her maiden voyage from London to India, being the first ever turbine steamer on the route. She became Hospital Ship No. 5 on 3 August 1914, with 80 doctors and 207 nurses. In 1915, she was sent to Gallipoli, bringing around 7,400 patients from the beaches and cliffs of the Dardanelles. At 11.15 p.m. on 4 January 1918, she was sunk in the Bristol Channel. Onboard were 279 walking wounded from Salonika. Only three Lascars, killed in the initial explosion, were lost and the remaining crew and passengers took to the boats. The crew and passengers were landed at Swansea.

One of the tragic hospital ship losses of the First World War was the *Rohilla*. She too had been requisitioned, this time on 6 August 1914, and was sent to Leith to be converted to a hospital ship. She had previously been converted into a semi-permanent troopship so conversion was relatively straightforward.

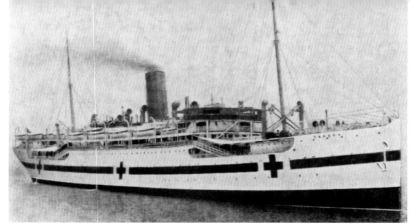

H.M. TROOPSHIP "ROHILLA."

Above left: Freshly painted in all-over white, with apple green stripe and red crosses, she sailed from Leith on 29 October, en route to Dunkirk and a shipload of wounded soldiers. Sailing inshore, she went aground off the Nab, Whitby, and became a total loss. Many of her crew managed to escape during the gale, thanks to the work of the Whitby, Upgang and Tynemouth lifeboats, but, despite clinging to the rigging, around eighty-three crew and medical staff were lost. This hand-painted postcard, done by a soldier aboard, shows the ship in her troopship livery *c.* 1910–2.

Above right: The BISNC liner *Takada* was one of a pair of sisters, both of which served as hospital ships and ambulance transports. Both were built by Alexander Stephen, of Linthouse, Glasgow, and completed in 1914. *Takada* trooped from Karachi to Marseilles in August 1914 and was converted to a hospital ship in June 1915. She had 450 beds and was to be found between Bombay, Karachi and Basra during the Mesopotamian campaign. She returned to service in April 1919. Her sister, *Tanda*, was taken over by the Government of India and used as a hospital ship, funded by the Madras War Fund. She was renamed *Madras* and could accommodate 450 patients and 102 medical staff. She became an ambulance transport at Vladivostok between June 1918 and November 1919. She reverted back to the name *Tanda* and was sunk by *U-181* near Mangalore in 1944.

HMHS *Vita* served in two world wars and although our photograph shows her as Hospital Ship No. 8 during the Second World War, she had an illustrious career in the first war too. Completed in October 1914, she was immediately pressed into war duty, sailing from Bombay to the Persian Gulf. She was converted into a hospital ship in 1916 and was equipped with 475 beds. In 1940 she was converted again into a hospital ship at Bombay and was based in Aden. She was bombed at Tobruk on 14 April 1941, being severely damaged. She was towed to Alexandria and, with a single engine in operation, made it to Bombay for repairs. She is shown here off Trincomalee, when she rescued crew from the sunken aircraft carrier *Hermes* and destroyer *Vampire* in April 1942.

CUNARD

Above left and right: At the start of the First World War, Cunard had three of Britain's largest merchant ships in the *Lusitania* and *Mauretania* of 1907 and the brand new *Aquitania*. Their ships were caught at various ports worldwide, and *Mauretania* had just left New York when war was declared. She raced to Halifax, where she eventually left on a dash for Liverpool. She is shown here arriving at Halifax before her dash across the North Atlantic and as she arrived in the Mersey after her first wartime voyage from Canada.

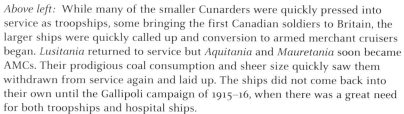

Above left: While many of the smaller Cunarders were quickly pressed into service as troopships, some bringing the first Canadian soldiers to Britain, the larger ships were quickly called up and conversion to armed merchant cruisers began. *Lusitania* returned to service but *Aquitania* and *Mauretania* soon became AMCs. Their prodigious coal consumption and sheer size quickly saw them withdrawn from service again and laid up. The ships did not come back into their own until the Gallipoli campaign of 1915–16, when there was a great need for both troopships and hospital ships.

Above right and below right: *Mauretania* in her distinctive dazzle-painted colour scheme.

Above left: Mauretania served in the Gallipoli campaign as both a troopship and a hospital ship. She is shown here coaling at Naples, which was a busy port once Italy entered the war, serving Allied shipping, which could use the natural harbour to refuel before the final voyage to the Dardanelles.

Above right: Mauretania at Naples, with Mount Vesuvius covered in mist.

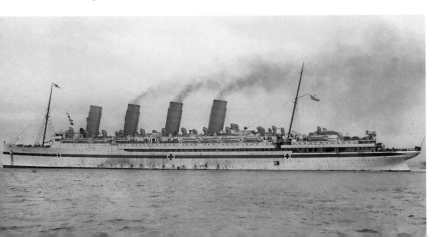

Mauretania with her coaling ports open at Naples.

A stern view of *Mauretania* as a hospital ship. The distinctive white livery was adorned with a green belt and red crosses, which were electrically lit at night.

Nurses aboard *Mauretania* at Naples, 1916. Many thousands of nurses were employed aboard the hospital ships, and although they entered war zones, the hospital ships were supposedly immune from attack by submarine or warship, even if they were not immune to the indiscriminate weapon of war that was the sea mine.

Mauretania would also use the ports of Brest and Marseille. In this censored view of 1916, she is shown leaving a 'French port'.

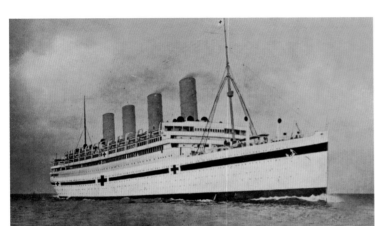

Aquitania was used for a very short time in 1914 as an armed merchant cruiser. She was introduced in May 1914 and made only three passenger voyages before war was declared in August. Her hunger for coal saw her withdrawn rather quickly. She, like *Mauretania*, was initially used as a troopship in the Dardanelles campaign, but heavy casualties saw both ships converted to hospital ships.

The famous marine artist Norman Wilkinson saw the landings at Gallipoli first-hand and he painted many views of the Allied attacks on the Turkish positions. *Aquitania* is shown here with a smaller hospital ship at her side.

Left: *Aquitania*, *Mauretania*, *Olympic* and *Britannic* were all too large to be risked close to the Dardanelles and all would call at Mudros, which was safer, and protected by elements of the Allied fleets.

Below: The wounded would be brought from the battlefront in smaller hospital ships and transferred to the larger vessels for onward shipment to hospitals in Britain. A Royal Mail Steam Packet ship has just left *Aquitania*'s starboard side, with another unloading her cargo of wounded soldiers on her port side.

The walking wounded would make their way up temporary gangplanks but the more seriously wounded and stretcher cases would be taken by medical auxiliaries from the wards of the smaller hospital ships to those of the large vessels.

The public rooms of the large ships were converted into wards, with the First Class rooms destined for officers and Second and Third Class public rooms for ordinary soldiers. As shown here, aboard *Aquitania*'s A Deck, much of the original panelling and artwork was left aboard ship during the work of transporting war-wounded soldiers.

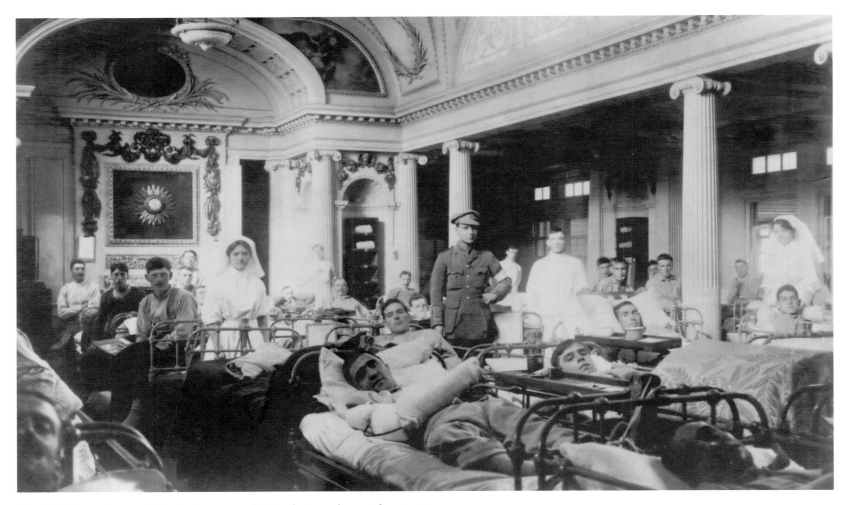

The A Deck main lounge of *Aquitania* as a ward. This photograph was taken at 4.50 p.m.

The two men in charge of HMHS *Aquitania*. Seated is her captain, C. A. Smith, and standing is Lt-Col. F. J. Brown of the Royal Army Medical Corps.

Trans-shipping wounded at sea just off Mudros. Behind *Aquitania*'s bow is the distinctive cupola of the Greek Orthodox church at Mudros.

The boat deck of *Aquitania*. After the loss of the *Titanic*, the rules on lifeboats changed and all ships had to carry enough lifeboats for all aboard. Carrying even more passengers as a troopship, much of *Aquitania*'s boat deck is crammed with lifeboats. Note the soldiers wearing life jackets, while the nurses are in their uniforms. Even in hospital ships, the danger of mines and even of sinking by submarines was a real threat.

ORIENT LINE

HMAT A5 *Omrah* leaving Port Melbourne on 10 October 1914, en route for Alexandria via Albany, Colombo and Suez. She was built by Fairfield's Govan yard in 1899 and was sunk on 12 May 1918, having been hit by a torpedo. She had been carrying troops of the 52nd and 74th divisions from Alexandria to Marseille, and was in convoy with six other transports on the return voyage.

HMAT *Orvieto* was the flagship of the only convoy she sailed in as a troopship. Built in 1909 at Workman, Clark's, Belfast, she is shown here at Port Melbourne on 19 October 1914. Later in the year, she was converted to a mine layer.

Above: Built in 1909 in Glasgow, the *Osterley* is shown in dazzle paint at the end of the war in November 1918. She is dressed overall in flags. In 1919 she returned to the Orient Line's service to Brisbane from Tilbury and was broken up in 1930.

Right: A censored postcard sent from the *Orvieto*.

ORIENT LINE
TO AUSTRALIA

s.s. *Orvieto*
Smoking Room

Head Offices—
FENCHURCH AVENUE
LONDON, E.C.

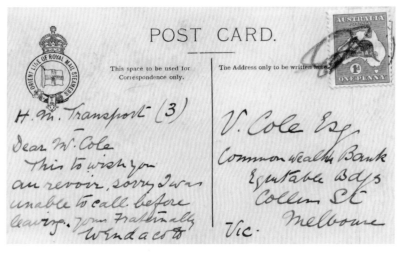

POST CARD.

This space to be used for
Correspondence only.

The Address only to be written here.

ONE PENNY

H. M. Transport (3)

Dear Mr Cole

This to wish you
au revoir, sorry I was
unable to call before
leaving. Yours Fraternally
Wendacott

V. Cole Esq.

Commonwealth Bank
Equitable Bdgs
Collins St
Vic.   Melbourne

Above and left: Sent by a soldier on board HMAT *Orvieto* in October or
November 1914, this is a pre-war postcard of the Smoking Room in First
Class.

Above left and above right: Two views of HMS *Orvieto*, taken about seven months apart in 1917–18, showing the different liveries she carried throughout the war. The right-hand image shows her in her dazzle paint scheme, designed to confuse the enemy as to the direction being travelled and the size of the vessel.

After beginning the war as an armed merchant cruiser, the *Orotava* ended her war as a troopship too. Here, she is loading Australian troops who are about to see their homes for the first time in five years. Built in 1889 for the Pacific Steam Navigation Company, she was managed by the Orient Line.

PENINSULAR & ORIENTAL STEAM NAVIGATION CO.

One of Britain's biggest shipping lines, P&O saw many of their vessels called up during the First World War. Built in 1899, the *Assaye* was designed for use as a troopship, ordinarily during the trooping season to Asia. She was used throughout the war as a hospital ship and was sold for scrap in 1928 in Stavanger, Norway.

Above: Built in 1896 at Harland & Wolff's, the *China* was nearly a total loss when she went ashore on Perim Island in 1898. She was salvaged after three months and rebuilt. She spent the war as a hospital ship. She was visited by King George V in June 1916 and scrapped in June 1928 in Japan, having been sold for £24,000.

Below: The *Delta* was built by Workman, Clark in their Belfast Queen's Island yard in 1905. She cost £159,783 to build and was destined for P&O's Eastern service. She became a hospital ship at Tsingtao in 1914, during the campaign to oust the Germans from the treaty ports on the Chinese coast. By 1919, she was a transport, taking troops back to Australia, and is shown here in Sydney in 1919.

Above: The *Dongola* was built by Barclay, Curle and entered service in 1905. She was primarily built for trooping to India. During the war, she was used in the Dardanelles as a hospital ship.

Right: In dry dock, the *Dongola* is getting her hull cleaned in preparation for repainting.

Above: *Dongola* as HMT No. 2. She cost £160,167 to build and in 1907 made a record run from Southampton to Bombay, taking a mere 18 days and 7 hours for the journey via the Suez Canal.

Right: Having spent a chunk of the war as a hospital ship, *Dongola* was quickly converted into a trooper to take Australians back to Western Australia. She is here at the end of one such voyage on 17 August 1919 at Fremantle, Western Australia.

Built in 1897, P&O's *Egypt* was used on Indian and Australasian services. She had cost £239,492 to build and in 1910 carried HRH the Princess Royal home from Egypt. She served from 1915 as HMHS *Egypt*, No. 52, and is shown here in that year at the Grand Harbour, Valetta, Malta.

Egypt entering Malta, being towed into the Grand Harbour by tug. Her hospital ship number, 52, is clearly visible at her bow.

Another view of HMHS Egypt. Egypt was lost in 1922 off Ushant, France. On 20 May that year she was in a collision with the French ship Seine and sank in 20 minutes. Gold bullion valued at £1,054,000 was lost, along with seventy-one crew and fifteen passengers. In 1930, the Italian salvage ship Artiglio brought up over £500,000 worth of gold from the deep wreck, using special diving suits and new salvage equipment that had never been used before.

H.M.T. KIMALAYA. AT. SOUTHAMPTON

The *Himalaya* was constructed in 1892 by Caird of Greenock. She was at the time of entering service the largest and fastest P&O ship, capable of 18 knots. Her first voyage to Sydney was a record breaking effort. In 1914, she was commissioned as an armed merchant cruiser at Penang and used in the Red Sea to guard the entrances to the Suez Canal. In 1916, the Admiralty purchased her and converted her to an aircraft carrier, with a squadron of seaplanes. She was based at East London, South Africa. In 1919, she returned to P&O and was used for trooping again. She is at Southampton trooping in the immediate post-war period in this photograph.

H M.T. KAISAR-I-HIND
In storm weather

Launched on 27 June 1914, *Kaiser-I-Hind* was the most expensive ship that P&O owned pre-war. She cost £363,176 and left on 1 October 1914 on her maiden voyage from London to Bombay, arriving in 17 days 20 hours and 52 minutes. In 1917, she was trooping, and escaped four torpedo attacks due to her high speed. One of the torpedoes actually hit her and failed to explode.

Some of the officers of HMS *Moldavia*, when she operated as an armed merchant cruiser. Built in 1900, she entered war service as an armed cruiser in 1915. On 23 May 1918, while carrying American troops, she was torpedoed off Beachy Head. She continued sailing on for fifteen minutes before she was stopped as she began to sink. Fifty-six crew and soldiers died as a result of the torpedo strike but everyone else was rescued by the escorting destroyers.

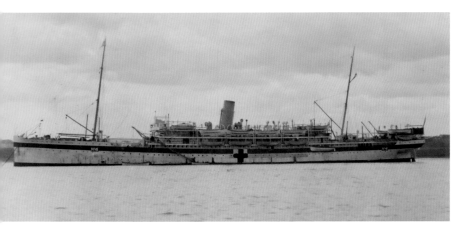

Left: Plassy was built in 1900 and was used almost exclusively for trooping. During the First World War, she was used as a hospital ship and is photographed here on the Firth of Forth during the war. She was scrapped in 1924.

Below left: Built for the Chinese service in 1901, *Somali* spent the war either trooping or as a hospital ship. In 1919, she was photographed at Sliema, still as a hospital ship, on 23 September that year.

Below right: Syria was built for trooping to India and Hong Kong and spent most of her career doing just that. She was broken up in 1924 by John Cashmore, a company that had numerous shipbreaking yards in Wales.

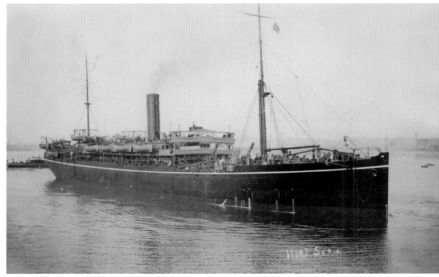

RAILWAY STEAMERS

Many British railway companies also owned ferries and paddle steamers. Those not entirely essential were called up for navy service. Many of the paddle steamers became minesweepers but a reasonable number of the screw steamers became vessels as diverse as seaplane carriers and minelayers. Some, especially those suited for the cross-Channel services, were used for trooping and as hospital ships. The London & North Western Railway's *Anglia* is here being utilised as a hospital ship.

The *Archangel* on prisoner repatriation duties on 17 November 1918, only six days after the end of the war. *Archangel* was a Great Eastern Railway steamer, sailing out of Harwich ordinarily, but she is shown here arriving into Hull with her load of Tommies.

The Great Eastern Railway's SS *Munich* was built in 1908 and was requisitioned as a hospital ship. Her name was changed in service to *St Denis* and when she was returned to the GER, she kept her new name. She was scuttled in Rotterdam in 1940 and was salvaged by the Germans to be used as an accommodation ship.

Built in 1908 by John Brown, Clydebank,
the *St Andrew* was fitted with three steam
turbines and was capable of 20 knots. She was
built especially for the Fishguard–Rosslare
service. On 19 August 1914, she was taken
up for military service and converted to
a hospital ship. She entered service on 24
August and made a journey to Rouen, where
she collected sixty-three stretcher cases and
147 other wounded soldiers. She remained on
cross-Channel work for most of her wartime
career. On 25 February 1915, she was chased
by the U-boat *U-8* near Boulogne but used
her speed to escape the slower submarine. By
November 1918, she was carrying both troops
and civilians, while still carrying the wounded
too.

A railway steamer at Boulogne as a hospital ship
in 1914. The ferries, used to quick turnarounds,
were ideal for the cross-Channel ambulance
ship crossings. This is the *St David* of the Great
Western Railway.

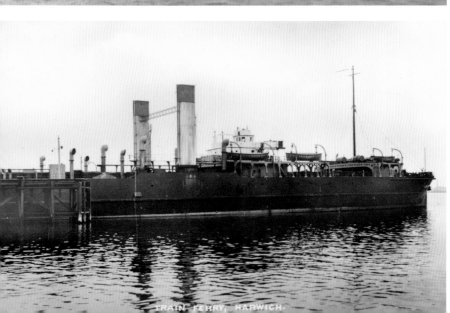

Above left: Taken up in 1914 for hospital ship duties, the *St David* remained on cross-Channel services for her military career. On 16 January 1919, she was released for refit. She was broken up at Cashmore's yard in Newport in September 1933.

Above right and below: A new military port was built at Richborough, near Thanet, Kent. The main ports of Ramsgate, Dover and Folkestone could not cope with the traffic heading for France. As well as weapons, munitions and stores, the ferries would occasionally carry hospital trains, ferrying the wounded back to the UK in a more unorthodox way.

ROYAL INDIAN MARINE SERVICE

The Royal Indian Marine Service built three troopships between 1900 and 1907. All three were built in the UK. The RIMS *Northbrook* entered service in 1907 and was built by John Brown at Clydebank. She is shown here at Britain's major trooping port of Southampton in 1907, prior to her maiden voyage to India.

Northbrook in dry dock at an Indian port. In 1914, she was converted to an armed vessel and spent much of the war in the Gulf and Red Sea.

Along with the *Northbrook*, the RIMS had two other vessels, *Dufferin* and *Hardinge*. *Hardinge* is shown here at sea immediately prior to the start of the First World War.

The RIMS *Hardinge* had primarily British officers with Indian crew. Her commander in 1910 was Captain St John, who is shown here with the officers of the ship.

In 1918, after a long period of little or no major maintenance, *Hardinge* was sailed to Hull, where she entered dry dock. The East African and Middle East campaigns were all but over as she had her funnels replaced.

Hardinge in dry dock at Hull in August 1918 with two of her nursing staff giving an idea of scale.

Two of *Hardinge*'s nurses pose in a lifeboat with an officer in the Persian Gulf in 1917.

The domestic staff of RIMS *Hardinge* in Hull, September 1918.

Hardinge would see the end of the war out in dock in Hull. On 11 November, the crew joined the victory parade in Hull and the Lascars paraded their tajah and a model of the ship they had sailed aboard since 1907.

With *Hardinge* in the background, the Chokras take a break as they dance into Hull from the docks for the victory parade. The seamen of RIMS *Hardinge* dressed in their finest uniforms to celebrate the end of the war.

ROYAL MAIL STEAM PACKET CO.

While not a troopship during the First World War, HMS *Almanzora* was completed by Harland & Wolff, Govan, in September 1915 and was hastily converted to an armed merchant cruiser. She spent much of the war with the 10th Cruiser Squadron, patrolling the sea lanes north of the UK. She is shown here, bristling with guns, on 30 May 1918. In 1939, she was converted to a troopship and spent most of the Second World War on this valuable duty.

Hospital Ship Araguaya

F0862, or HMHS *Araguaya*, was built by Harland & Wolff for the Royal Mail Steam Packet Co. and launched on 5 June 1906. In 1914, she remained in commercial service and became a hospital ship in 1917. Painted here in a dazzle paint scheme rather than all-over white, she is shown that year in Halifax, Nova Scotia. In all, she made nineteen voyages for the Canadians. She was used until 1920, when she was returned to commercial service on 9 October.

Below: Two views of RMS *Arcadian*, the first showing her as a troopship at Marseille, the second showing the result of a German torpedo on 15 April 1917. She had begun life as the Pacific Steam Navigation Co.'s RMS *Ortona* in 1899 and was used as a trooper to South Africa in 1902 as Transport No. 112. Bought by RMSP and converted to a cruise ship in 1910, she was then renamed *Arcadian*. In 1915, she had become a troopship and was the headquarters ship for Sir Ian Hamilton at Gallipoli. When she was torpedoed, she was carrying 1,335 troops and crew, of whom around 279 died. In the rather dramatic view of her going down by the head, you can clearly see troops jumping into the water and dangling from ropes and each black dot in the water is the head of a man, left to drown by the crew of a German submarine.

R.M.S. ARCADIAN

A British Transport Beached   © I.F.S.
From N. Moser, N.Y.

In this doctored image, used in America for publicity
purposes just as the US entered the war, we can see more
clearly the men scrambling for their lives, the lifeboat the
original photograph was taken from being doctored to show
the ship aground.

Asturias was the fifth of a set of ships built for Royal Mail in
1907. She made her maiden voyage between London and Brisbane
on 24 January 1908. Asturias then began to ply her trade from
Southampton to the River Plate. She was one of the first ships to be
requisitioned, on 1 August 1914, as a hospital ship.

Left: While on cross-Channel service between Le Havre and Southampton, she was nearly torpedoed by a German submarine on the surface. The U-boat missed but the event was captured on this propaganda postcard issued immediately after the event.

Below: A view of RMS *Asturias* early in the war as HMHS No. 2.

Above: The hospital ship *Asturias* at Southampton, berthed at the entrance to the White Star Dock. On 20 March 1917, she was not so lucky and was torpedoed, with her stern blown off as a result. She managed to make her way to Bolt Head, where she was beached. Despite being in full hospital ship colours, thirty-five crew and medics lost their lives when she was hit. She was towed to port and became an ammunition hulk at Plymouth, having been purchased by the Admiralty. With a shortage of ships at the end of the war, and with British shipyards busy building new vessels, *Asturias* was repurchased by Royal Mail and laid up in Belfast in preparation for a two-year rebuild. She emerged in 1923 as RMS *Arcadian*, and replaced the earlier cruise ship *Arcadian*, lost in 1917.

Below: Built for both cruising and inter-island service in the West Indies, RMS *Berbice* was a much smaller ship, grossing 2,379 grt. She was a mere 300 feet long and was launched from the Queen's Island yard of Harland & Wolff on 6 May 1909, entering service soon afterwards.

The *Berbice* was used throughout the war as a hospital ship.

Shown here at a British port towards the end of the war, *Berbice* sparkles in her white livery. At her bow is a paravane, used to cut the wires of mines and prevent them from damaging the ship. Mines were an indiscriminate weapon, recognising neither friend nor foe, nor even distinguishing between hospital ships and warships.

Above and below: Two views of HMHS *Drina*, Hospital Ship No. 3. Built in Belfast as the last of a series of five ships, she became one of the first ships to be requisitioned as a hospital ship on 1 August 1914. She was returned to commercial service in 1915 but was torpedoed and sunk off Milford Haven, Pembrokeshire, by the U-boat *UC-65*. Her remains lie off Skokholm island. Fifteen lost their lives in the sinking.

UNION-CASTLE LINE

Braemar Castle was the last four-masted ship built for the Castle Line and was constructed by Barclay, Curle in 1898. In 1909, she was used for trooping to the Far East. At the start of the First World War, she was used to take elements of the British Expeditionary Force to France on 6 August 1914. In March 1915, she took the Plymouth Brigade of the Royal Marines to Gallipoli, landing them at Siddil-Bahr in April. Making numerous other trooping voyages, she was then converted into a hospital ship and commissioned on 7 October 1915.

Equipped with 421 beds, HMHS *Braemar Castle* acted as a base hospital ship at Mudros, and when full, she left for Italy to unload her cargo of wounded troops. On 23 November 1916, she struck a mine in the Mykonos Channel, with the loss of six patients. She was towed to Malta and left for three months. She was repaired and re-entered service at La Spezia. In March 1918, she was sailed to Murmansk with the British force that occupied this part of Russia to prevent capture of Russian weapons and ammunition by the Germans. She remained for nearly a year as base hospital. In February 1919, she sailed for Leith, carrying wounded. In 1921, she returned to Archangel to evacuate sick, wounded and non-Russians from the port. She was the last ship to leave and thus made the last hospital ship voyage that was a consequence of the First World War. In all, over 2,655,000 wounded had been carried by hospital ships during the war and its aftermath.

Above: Built for the Union Line by Harland & Wolff in 1897, *Briton* was the third ship to carry the name. She carried 1,500 troops to the Boer War in 1897. On 27 August 1914, she left Cape Town in convoy for the UK with five other Union-Castle liners, carrying 4,000 troops. *Briton* remained in commercial service for much of the war but her Third Class accommodation was primarily used for troops. In 1915, she made several voyages carrying mainly troops and was used for the Gallipoli campaign too. In February 1918, she carried Nigerian troops between Mombasa and Lagos, as shown here, and then sailed for New York to bring a shipload of doughboys to Europe. She was scrapped in 1926.

Left: Carisbrook Castle was built in 1898 at Fairfield's yard at Govan, Glasgow. She was commissioned as a hospital ship on 3 September 1914, having been commandeered by the Admiralty on 2 August 1914. She had accommodation for 439 patients. Her initial service was cross-Channel but she was too big for the small number of patients and was converted into a troopship for 1,500. In January 1915, she trooped to Alexandria and carried a Canadian field hospital to Salonika, Greece. She spent a part of the year trooping between Salonica, Mudros and Alexandria.

In 1918, *Carisbrook Castle* was used as a cross-Channel troop ferry but also as an Australian troop transport, as shown here. In 1919, she was again used in the Mediterranean as an ambulance transport before reverting to company service on 26 August 1919.

Above: Built in 1911, *Gloucester Castle* was commissioned on 24 September 1914 as a hospital ship with beds for 410 patients. In 1915, she was used as a troopship in the Gallipoli campaign, carrying the Portsmouth Battalion of the Royal Marines. On 30 March 1917, despite being in hospital ship livery, she was torpedoed by *UB-32* in the English Channel while travelling between Le Havre and Southampton. Three died during the evacuation. The ship herself was not mortally wounded and was taken to Portsmouth after salvage. She was returned to Union-Castle on 9 April 1919 and was sunk in 1942 by a commerce raider off Ascension Island.

Below: Completed at Barclay, Curle, Glasgow, in 1910, *Grandtully Castle* was an intermediate steamer of 7,612 grt. She was initially used as a troopship, seeing service at Gallipoli, where she and five other troopships left Mudros on 18 March 1915. Because of mines, the ships did not land their troops until 23 April. On 1 May 1915, she left the war zone for Malta and was commissioned as HMHS *Grandtully Castle* on 22 June, with accommodation for 552 patients. On 11 March 1919, she returned to Union-Castle and was broken for scrap in 1939.

Completed in 1899, *Kildonan Castle*'s maiden voyage was as a troopship during the Boer War. She carried 3,000 troops from Southampton to Cape Town, arriving on 18 October 1899. On 31 October 1914, she sailed to Lisbon to load 10,000 rifles and a million rounds of ammunition for South Africa. Arriving back in Southampton on 21 November 1914, she was then commissioned as a hospital ship on 6 October 1915, with room for 603 beds. In 1916, she became an armed merchant cruiser and in 1917 took the British Military Mission to Russia from Oban to Murmansk. In December 1918, she was paid off as an AMC, and repatriated troops through 1919. In 1919, she also saw service at Archangel, taking British troops there, and made a single voyage to Shanghai as a trooper. Her war service ended in 1920, when she took 1,600 Yugoslav refugees from Vladivostok to the Adriatic.

Entering service in January 1914, *Llandovery Castle* was almost brand new when war occurred. She remained in commercial service until 26 July 1916, when she was commissioned as a hospital ship for 622 patients, with 102 medical staff. She was used by the Canadian army. On 27 June 1918, she became Union-Castle's last casualty of the war. Fully illuminated, her red crosses and white hull visible for miles, she was torpedoed by *U-86* when en route from Halifax to Liverpool. She was 118 miles from Fastnet with 258 crew and medical staff aboard. After she was sunk, *U-86* surfaced and shelled and machine-gunned the crew in the boats with the loss of 234, including eighty-eight medical staff. There had been ninety-four nurses aboard and many died that day. Only one lifeboat escaped and the twenty-four crew were picked up by HMS *Lysander*. Two of the officers of U-86 were jailed for war crimes.

WHITE STAR LINE

The White Star Line, although majority American-owned, was a British registered company and all their ships were, at the time, registered in Liverpool. They saw many vessels called up for service as armed merchant cruisers, including their first to be built under government subsidy to be converted to a warship in time of need. Although not used as either a troopship or hospital ship, *Teutonic* served as an armed merchant cruiser and her officers are shown here in 1916.

Olympic, the line's largest ship in service at the start of the First World War, was still in passenger service in October 1914 when she went to the aid of the navy battlecruiser HMS *Audacious*, which had hit a mine off Lough Swilly. The *Olympic*'s lifeboats rescued many of the crew and because of the danger of mines, the *Olympic* sailed for the Clyde rather than Liverpool, where she is shown here at Gourock, being tendered by the Caledonian Steam Packet Company's paddle steamer PS *Duchess of Fife*.

Olympic at Mudros. Armed with guns at her bow and stern, she has dulled-down grey upper works as she lies at anchor in the bay. Many soldiers crowd her A and B decks as they await trans-shipment to either Mudros itself or onto ships for the short journey to the Dardanelles.

For a short time, the largest of the troopships were not required. Both *Mauretania* and *Olympic* were laid up on the Clyde for a period. These three views, taken from a British submarine, show the *Olympic* laid up in the relative safety of the Firth of Clyde.

Right: Another view of *Olympic* on the Clyde, showing her B deck almost fully enclosed. Her guns have been removed.

Below: *Olympic* on the Clyde.

Left: As conditions worsened in both France and the Mediterranean, *Olympic* was required to bring Canadian troops from Halifax, Nova Scotia. Photographed from her poop deck, we get some nice detail of her Stothert & Pitt-built cranes, as well as of the thousands of Canadian troops aboard.

Below: *Olympic* at Halifax in 1916. At this time, she was armed with open 4-inch guns. Later in the war, she would be fitted with more and larger guns, veritably bristling with them.

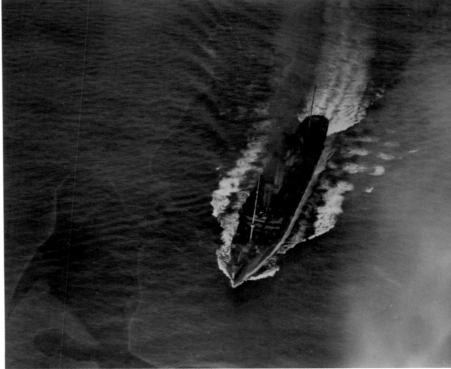

Above: Photographed on 16 August 1918, *Olympic* travels up the Solent at speed on a return trip from Canada.

Left: Olympic in her rather dramatic dazzle colour scheme at Southampton sometime in late 1917.

Above: Shuttling backwards and forwards across the Atlantic, *Olympic* was used for training purposes by aerial photographers of the fledgling RAF, flying from their base at Weymouth. This view shows *Olympic* on 3 September 1918 in the Solent from 1,000 feet.

Left: With a destroyer escort, *Olympic* travels towards Southampton on 21 September 1918, photographed from a seaplane at 1,500 feet.

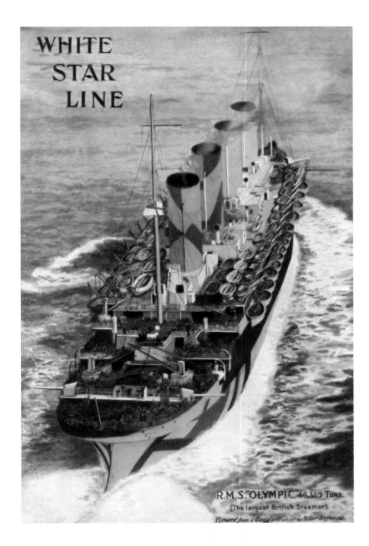

Above: As the war ended, *Olympic* was used to transport tens of thousands of Canadian soldiers back home. Many had fond memories of the ship that had brought them to Europe and brought many of them safely back home.

Left: The prime result of all of this aerial photography was one of the most famous views of *Olympic*, this colour photograph, used as a company-issued postcard, and also as a poster.

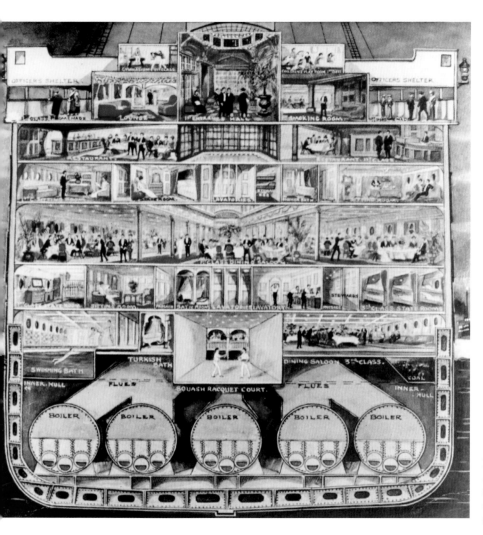

In February 1914, White Star Line launched their biggest ship, the RMS *Britannic*. The ship was due to enter service later in 1914, but work slowed as the crisis in Europe escalated into full-blown war. The ship lay partially completed as the war ravaged Europe, but the needs of the Gallipoli campaign saw her requisitioned as a hospital ship.

Britannic would make six voyages between Southampton and Mudros, and is shown here at the Greek island trans-shipping wounded soldiers. The hospital ship at her side gives an idea of the sheer size of Britain's largest vessel.

Britannic in Southampton Water, 1916. *Britannic* was fitted with specially designed davits that could launch around six lifeboats each. She was also fitted with a second skin, making her both wider and safer than her sister *Titanic*.

Enterprising postcard publishers would stock the ship up in Southampton and these postcards would be sold to the returning soldiers, who would have nothing better to do than write back home. This is the original artwork for one such artist-drawn postcard.

Another postcard of *Britannic*, from 1916.

These postcards were very realistic, as shown by the comparison between this bow shot and the photograph of *Britannic* shown in the next view.

Left: *Britannic* at Southampton being coaled in the Ocean Dock. Her official number at this time was G08. The small two-funnelled hospital ship to her left is D68 while on the extreme left, at berth 43, is the *Aquitania.*

Below: *Britannic* looking rather war-weary and battered, with her paint all dull and worn.

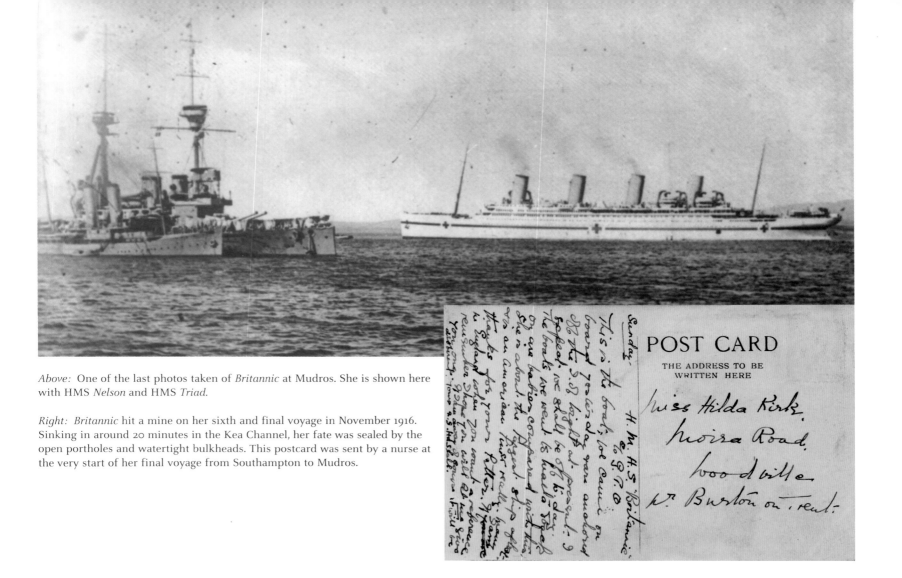

Above: One of the last photos taken of *Britannic* at Mudros. She is shown here with HMS *Nelson* and HMS *Triad.*

Right: *Britannic* hit a mine on her sixth and final voyage in November 1916. Sinking in around 20 minutes in the Kea Channel, her fate was sealed by the open portholes and watertight bulkheads. This postcard was sent by a nurse at the very start of her final voyage from Southampton to Mudros.

POST CARD

THE ADDRESS TO BE
WRITTEN HERE

Miss Hilda Kirk.
Moira Road.
Woodville.
Nr. Burton on Trent.

After the loss of *Lusitania* in May 1915, Cunard expected to be given a new ship then being built at Harland & Wolff. The new vessel was originally to have been Holland America Line's *Statendam*, but was instead launched as *Justicia*. After the loss of the *Britannic*, and because White Star had a spare crew available, the ship was transferred to them.

Justicia made numerous voyages as a troopship before being torpedoed on 19–20 July 1918. She was hit by six torpedoes, four from *UB-64* and two from *UB-124*.

White Star would also manage the SS *Zeppelin*, which would be used as an American troopship, taking 15,800 American troops back home at the end of the war.

Above: The Donaldson liner *Saturnia* was launched in 1910 and used as a troopship for the Dardanelles campaign in 1915. She took Canadian wounded back afterwards.

Opposite: Marseille's location meant that the port was busy, both for ships travelling to the Mediterranean and Egypt, but also as a repair facility too, for those ships that had been damaged or needed refitted. The Anchor Line's *Transylvania* was introduced in 1914 and was called up for troopship service later that year. In 1917, she was overhauled at Marseille and left there on 3 May for Alexandria with 200 officers and over 2,800 men. In the Gulf of Genoa the next day, she was hit by a submarine and sank with the loss of 414.

The sister of *Saturnia* was the *Letitia*, built by Scotts at Greenock. She was converted into a hospital ship but was lost when she went ashore at Portuguese Cove, Chebucto Head, Nova Scotia, on 1 August 1917. The crew and passengers were all saved but the ship was a total loss.

The *St Margaret of Scotland* was staffed by Scottish doctors, nurses and orderlies because the country had raised £22,000 to equip her. The Scots had been very generous when it came to hospital ships, ambulance boats and ambulances, providing tens of thousands of pounds to supply and equip these vital things.

The Mesopotamian campaign focused on the Tigris and Euphrates rivers, with much movement of troops and of wounded by launch and river boat. *Silver Thimble VI* was one of a series of motor boats paid for by the Scots to transport the wounded quickly and comfortably down the rivers from the battlefields.

A river steamer, PA7, used at Baghdad to transport troops. Similar river boats were painted in hospital ship colours too.

The Aberdeen Steam Navigation Company's *Aberdonian* was converted into a hospital ship and used between 1915 and 1919. Built by D. & W. Henderson at Glasgow, she was 264 feet in length.

Many of the Bibby liners were used as troopships during the First World War. The most famous was perhaps the 1912 *Oxfordshire*. She was one of the first hospital ships to be requisitioned and became No. 1. She went to Scapa Flow but was too large for the needs there and was transferred to cross-Channel work and then to the Dardanelles, where she became the base ship at Mudros. She was involved in the ANZAC withdrawal from there.

Left: Decommissioned on 24 March 1919, *Oxfordshire* had carried 50,000 wounded soldiers and steamed 172,000 miles on 235 voyages. The 50,000 men she had carried was the largest number of any hospital ship of the war.

Below: Built in 1897, the *Derbyshire* served from January 1915 as a troopship. In 1917, she was used by the Americans to bring troops to Europe. Post-war, she continued as a troopship until the late 1920s.

Right: The Blue Funnel Line's SS *Ascanius* taking the South Australian Infantry to Europe on 20 October 1914 as HMAT A11.

Below: *Ascanius* was used by the Australians for numerous voyages. This one, from Melbourne, was her fourteenth convoy, and she carried the 8th Infantry Brigade, part of the 11th Reinforcements and 12th Infantry Battalion via Suez and Port Said to Alexandria.

"S.S. ASCANIUS."
Departure of South Australian Infantry
of the First Australian Expeditionary Force
from Outer Harbour S.A. 20ᵗʰ October 1914.

The Atlantic Transport Line's SS *Minnetonka* as a troopship at Marseille.

When the larger ships pulled into Southampton docks, it was found to be easier to use smaller hospital yachts to take the wounded to Netley Hospital, further down the Solent. Soldiers on a smaller hospital boat are seen passing the Royal Pier in Southampton, with a Red Funnel paddle steamer behind.

The steam yacht *Liberty* at Cowes on 27 August 1914. Purchased by Lord Tredegar in 1914, she was requisitioned as a hospital yacht in 1915. She was Hospital Ship No. 10 and was often found on patrol in the North Sea under the command of Lord Tredegar.

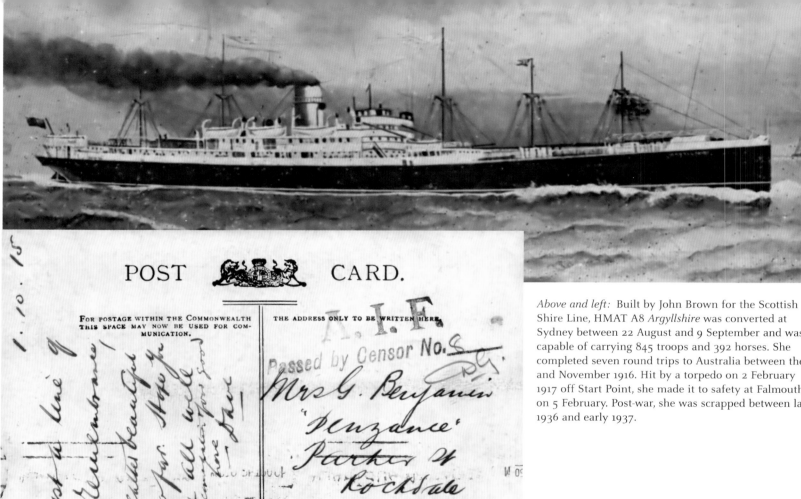

1.10.15

A. I. F.

Passed by Censor No. 9

Just a line of
remembrance
weather beautiful
hope we
are all well
A line from front later

Mrs G. Benjamin
"Penzance"
Parker St
Rockdale

Above and left: Built by John Brown for the Scottish Shire Line, HMAT A8 *Argyllshire* was converted at Sydney between 22 August and 9 September and was capable of carrying 845 troops and 392 horses. She completed seven round trips to Australia between then and November 1916. Hit by a torpedo on 2 February 1917 off Start Point, she made it to safety at Falmouth on 5 February. Post-war, she was scrapped between late 1936 and early 1937.

Above and right: The Federal Steam Navigation Company's *Shropshire* was HMAT A9. The top view shows the *Shropshire* leaving Melbourne on convoy 24. The bottom view shows her leaving Melbourne on 11 May 1917 on convoy 31.

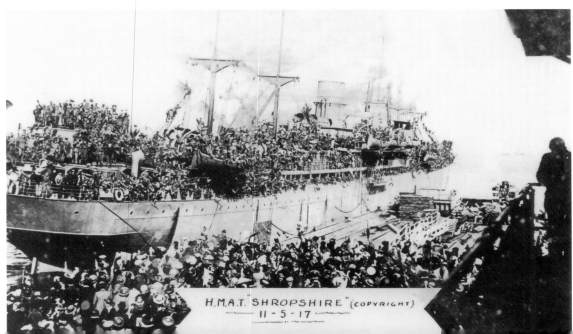

H.M.A.T. SHROPSHIRE (COPYRIGHT) 11-5-17

Hospital ships in the Aegean in 1915 by famed marine artist Norman Wilkinson RI.

463 Cap Polonio. 18 7 19

The ex-Hamburg-Sud Amerika liner *Cap Polonio* as a trooper in 1919.

Captured German and Austrian ships, the *Huntsgreen*, *Huntsend* and *Huntspill* were used as troopers throughout the war.

Above: The Dutch steamer *Orange Nassau* at Tilbury with exchanged prisoners of war. The Dutch were neutral and their ships were often used to repatriate severely injured or mentally incapacitated soldiers.

Below: The German liner *Melilla* with repatriated British prisoners of war.

MUIRHEAD BONE, WAR ARTIST

Muirhead Bone was thirty-eight when he became an official war artist. He was sent to France to capture the realism of war, so that there would be a record post-war of the terrible conflict. These six images help show life aboard and alongside a hospital ship, with many of the images drawn at Marseille, with its distinctive transporter bridge.